SNOW LEO

illustrated by Lynne Cherry

Methuen Children's Books

It is cold
high up
where the snow leopards live.

Their coats are thick.
Their tails are long and furry.

Their spots help to hide them in the rocks.

Mother jumps.
Baby jumps.
Young ones learn...

to wait…to watch…to hunt alone
in their high mountain home.

for Michael Cherry,
a snow leopard who has been reincarnated
as my little brother

First published in Great Britain in 1987
by Methuen Children's Books Ltd
11 New Fetter Lane, London EC4P 4EE

Published in the United States by E P Dutton, New York
Text copyright © 1987 E P Dutton
Illustrations copyright © 1987 Lynne Cherry

Printed in Singapore by Tien Wah Press
All rights reserved
Licensed by World Wildlife Fund

ISBN 0 416 03032 7